Original title:
Threads of Art

Copyright © 2024 Swan Charm Publishing
All rights reserved.

Editor: Jessica Elisabeth Luik
Author: Kene Elistrand
ISBN HARDBACK: 978-9916-86-148-6
ISBN PAPERBACK: 978-9916-86-149-3

Inked Fabric

Threads of black on linen white,
With every stroke, a timeless fight.
A tapestry of thought revealed,
In every script, a world concealed.

Patterns form from heart and hand,
Written tales across the land.
Each letter dances, deft and sly,
A canvas where the ink can fly.

Waves of prose in twilight's glow,
A river where the words will flow.
Stitches of a mind set free,
Inked fabric tells our history.

Harmonic Weavings

Notes like threads in music's loom,
A melody in twilight's bloom.
Harmony in every strand,
An orchestra at our command.

Strings and brass with voices blend,
A symphony that never ends.
Each refrain, a woven dream,
A song that sails on every stream.

Rhythmic beats like footfalls light,
Guiding dancers through the night.
Harmonic weavings tie us close,
In music's realm, we find repose.

Woven Murals

Colors spread on canvas wide,
With every brush, our worlds collide.
Each hue a tale, each shade a dream,
Woven murals make hearts gleam.

Stories bold in every stroke,
From sunset gold to cloudy cloak.
Scenes of life in vibrant form,
Art that keeps our spirits warm.

Textures rich, a feast for eyes,
In painted skies, the soul relies.
Woven murals, silent yet clear,
Speak of love and every fear.

Coded Colors

In a screen's soft gleam, hues intertwine,
Whispers of red, blue, pixels align.
Patterns of passion, cold data's flair,
Silent symphonies, coded with care.

Green mixes knowledge with hope's desire,
Yellow flares bright as sunlit fire.
In binary streams, life's hues unfold,
Mystic tapestry, coded in bold.

Veils of Light

Morning dew drapes on blades so fine,
Refracting rays, a dance divine.
Veils of light in the dawn's embrace,
Unveil a world, soft and graced.

Evening shadows stretch and weave,
Golden flares the sky receives.
Night draws nearer, stars ignite,
Veils of dark, stitched with light.

Threaded Masterpieces

Needles dance with threads of lore,
Crafting tales, legends of yore.
Each stitch a whisper, a dream's quest,
Threaded seams, hearts expressed.

Colors blend, a woven trance,
Fabric sighs, a soft romance.
Masterpieces, each thread aligns,
Artistry in patterns, fine designs.

Vivid Quilts

Patches of memories, vibrant and grand,
Stitched with love by a gentle hand.
Each square a story, laughter or tear,
Vivid quilts hold lives so dear.

Warmth in layers, histories spun,
Blankets of past and futures begun.
Colors burst in a radiant parade,
Quilts of dreams, timelessly made.

Threaded Chronicles

In the loom of time, threads intertwine,
Crafting tales in fibers fine.
Moments stitch with hands unseen,
Weaving patterns softly keen.

History's tapestries unfold,
Every strand a story told.
Whispers of past, future's call,
In this weave, we're one and all.

Colors fade and sometimes blend,
In each twist, beginnings end.
Yet in this rich, textured dome,
Every thread finds its home.

Tissued Dreams

In the folds of silken night,
Tissued dreams take trembling flight.
Moonlight weaves through shadowed seams,
Softly stitching fragile dreams.

Whispers float on twilight breeze,
Tales of wonder, whispered pleas.
In this realm of sleep's embrace,
Dreams find form and gentle grace.

Morning comes with golden ray,
Tissues fade in light of day.
Yet the dreams, though shadows seem,
Leave a mark in heart's own beam.

Crafted Hues

Brush on canvas, strokes of life,
Crafted hues in moments rife.
Colors blend and stories bloom,
In this art, we find our room.

Each shade tells a whispered tale,
Hues that dance and never pale.
In the silence of the frame,
Life and light are one and same.

Through each brush, a soul's delight,
Crafted hues in day and night.
In this masterpiece so grand,
Heart and art go hand in hand.

Woven Realities

Threads of time in hand of fate,
Woven worlds anticipate.
In the pattern, truth unfurls,
Life in weft and warp of pearls.

Reality's rich, woven strand,
Crafted by a mindful hand.
Every twist and turn reveals,
The fabric of our hopes and deals.

Seen and unseen, threads align,
Weaving dreams and time divine.
In this woven world's grand scheme,
Life is more than it may seem.

Kaleidoscope Weave

Colors dance, a vibrant thread
Through the fabric, swiftly spread
Patterns shifting, hues agleam
Knitting worlds within a dream.

Every stitch, a story spins
Chromatic tales on silken pins
Fractured light in fabric form
Weaving through a heart so warm.

Threads of gold and spectral light
Interlace, dispel the night
A tapestry of endless scope
Crafted in a kaleidoscope.

Crafted Echoes

Whispered winds through ancient halls
Elders' tales within these walls
Voices born in rhythmic flow
Echoes crafted, long ago.

Silent whispers in the thread
Words unspoken, softly said
Loom of time, a gentle weave
Crafts a tale we all believe.

Songs of ages, woven tight
Craft the echoes of the night
In the silence, stories ring
Crafted echoes, pure they sing.

Bursting Looms

Threads of tension, woven tight
Bursting forth in rays of light
Fabric teems with vibrant bloom
Life erupts from bursting loom.

Patterns pulsing, bold, alive
In this weave, the spirits thrive
Every thread a joy consumes
Energy from bursting looms.

Waves of color, bright and free
Bursting forth from you and me
Threads entwined in fateful spindles
Create wonder as they mingle.

Variegated Dreams

Dreams of color, dreams of light
Spun in threads of dark and bright
Woven tight by moonbeam beams
Crafting variegated dreams.

Nightly realms where shadows play
Threads of silver, threads of grey
Weaving moments, soft and tender
In a dream of mixed-up splendor.

Every slumber, fabrics dive
In the loom, our spirits thrive
Woven whispers, dreams conceived
In the cloth, our dreams achieved.

Spun Mosaics

Threads of color wove the light,
In patterns bold and subtly bright.
Night and day in fabric spun,
Under moon and morning sun.

Fragments dance in poised array,
Echoes of a dawnlit day.
Silent whispers clad in hues,
Gather in a twilight muse.

Stories painted, line by line,
Fusing realms of space and time.
Tapestries of dreams respire,
Born of breath and woven fire.

Mingled Media

Brush and ink in fluid streams,
Blend of truths and fleeting dreams.
Digital meets dusk and dawn,
Borders blurred, a world reborn.

Pixelated hearts reflect,
Melded shapes that intersect.
Canvas yields to code and clay,
Art redefined in modern sway.

Prints and pulses, veins of light,
Chasing shadows into night.
Echoed rhythms, blend again,
Art transcends the human pen.

Whispers in Canvas

Silent strokes on woven field,
Secrets spoken, truths revealed.
Softest murmurs in the grain,
Colors spill like autumn rain.

Minds entwined in painted thread,
Canvas caught what words unsaid.
Echoes tinged in twilight glaze,
Frozen in a painter's daze.

Each whisper found in subtle hue,
A story old, forever new.
Unfolding in a timeless trance,
A dance of quiet happenstance.

Palette of Dreams

Shades of reverie in flight,
Chasing moonbeams through the night.
Brushes dipped in twilight streams,
Craft a world from painter's dreams.

Velvet skies and stardust trails,
Sun-kissed whispers, morn unveils.
Every hue a tale unfolds,
In a realm where sight beholds.

Dreams are spun in vibrant space,
Touching realms of boundless grace.
Colors weave a night's delight,
Waking visions, taking flight.

Stitched Stories

Threads of fate in fabric sewn,
Tales of old and futures known.
Needles dance through cloth rainbowed,
Lives interlace, spirits grow.

Looms of time weave joy and tears,
Stitched memories, through the years.
Every patch, a new tale shown,
Worlds within the seams are known.

Hands that sew, with love imbued,
Each small piece, a life's prelude.
In every quilt, histories flow,
Stitched stories that hearts bestow.

Braided Perceptions

Visions twist in threads of thought,
Dreams and truths intricately caught.
In each braid, a secret sought,
Perceptions blend as they ought.

Strands of light and shadow play,
Forming dawn and dusk's display.
Through these twists, our minds convey,
Life's own tale in woven array.

Braided paths that intertwine,
Hearts and minds in braided line.
Through this art, we redefine,
Our world's view, so intertwined.

Myriad Strokes

Sweeps of ink on paper vast,
Moments captured, shadows cast.
In each line, a time that's past,
Stories drawn to ever last.

Brushes whisper, voices heard,
Silent songs in every word.
Myriad strokes, emotions spurred,
Canvas speaks where hearts are stirred.

Artistry, in brush's sweep,
Depths of thought, both wide and deep.
Through each stroke, our visions keep,
Echoes of dreams, where shadows leap.

Textured Epiphanies

In woven dreams of muted tones,
We find the heartstrings of our bones.
Each flaw, a gem of raw delight,
In shadows cast by moonlit night.

Threads that tell of days gone by,
A tapestry beneath the sky.
Whispered secrets, softly blend,
In every start, a humble end.

Patterns twine in subtle hues,
Like fleeting thoughts we seldom choose.
Each knot, a memory to keep,
In textured silence, secrets seep.

Awakened by the break of dawn,
Epiphanies on cloth are drawn.
In every stitch, a story lives,
A wordless gift the fiber gives.

Stitched Whispers

In every seam, a tale of old,
Through silken threads, the past unfolds.
Soft murmurs from the cloth arise,
Beneath the hands, a whispered guise.

In gentle loops, emotions weave,
A silent song, one can't conceive.
The needle's path, a dancer's grace,
Leaves whispers in its gentle trace.

Each fabric speaks in tones subdued,
Of joy and sorrow, meek and crude.
An unvoiced hymn, a tender plea,
In every weave, a sight to see.

The needle's kiss on woven lips,
In heartbeats felt through fingertips.
A symphony of soft replies,
In stitched whispers, love resides.

Clever Tangles

In tangled webs of truths and lies,
The clever threads, they twist and rise.
They turn and knot in clever ways,
A dance of yarn in night and days.

Through every twist, a story's spun,
In every tangle, there's begun.
A clever maze of thoughts entwined,
In clever tangles, seek and find.

The yarns they weave in intricate shades,
In clever tangles, a journey wades.
A path obscure, yet clear in kind,
Mysteries in tangles defined.

Through every knot and loop and snare,
A lesson learned, a truth laid bare.
In clever tangles, our lives unfold,
A labyrinth of tales untold.

Fiber Fantasies

In threads of dreams, our spirits soar,
Through fantasies of cloth and more.
Every thread, a tale untold,
A world of wonder to behold.

The fibers weave a magic land,
Where hopes and dreams meet hand in hand.
Imagination, wildly free,
In woven dreams of what might be.

Colors blend in splendid hue,
Creating realms both old and new.
Each stitch a longing, wild and deep,
In fiber fantasies, secrets sleep.

Embark on journeys great and grand,
In woven tales and lands unplanned.
Through fiber threads, the heart does see,
A universe of fantasy.

Brushstrokes of Time

A canvas stretched across the years,
Where dreams and hopes align,
Each stroke a whisper soft and clear,
Through morning's gentle shine.

The past and future softly blend,
In hues both bright and dim,
An artist's hand our hearts suspend,
On life's broad, painted rim.

With every sweep, life's stories told,
In colors bold and new,
The secrets in the brush unfold,
A tale both old and true.

Moments caught in fleeting grace,
On textures rich and fair,
Time's tender touch we all embrace,
In art beyond compare.

Eternal strokes on fleeting days,
An endless, timeless climb,
Our souls are painted in arrays,
By brushstrokes of our time.

Interwoven Colors

Threads of crimson, threads of gold,
Intertwining tales are spun,
Stories whispered, stories told,
Underneath the setting sun.

Emerald greens and sapphire blues,
Merge in vibrant, living streams,
Painting life with varied hues,
Weaving through our hopes and dreams.

Every line and every shade,
Crafts a tapestry so wide,
In the interwoven parade,
Where all our memories reside.

Shadows dance and lights converge,
In a kaleidoscope's embrace,
Colors rise and colors surge,
Defining time and space.

Hand in hand, the fibers weave,
Binding lives in chromatic tether,
In the pattern we believe,
That binds our hearts together.

Symphony in Oil

In vivid strokes, the canvas sings,
A melody of light and shade,
Echoes of the painter's strings,
In colors deftly laid.

The brush a maestro's wand of grace,
Each stroke a note unheard,
Creating symphonies that trace,
A world without a word.

Textures rich with depth and hue,
Compose a silent song,
Through valleys steep and skies so blue,
With tones both bold and strong.

Silent harmonies arise,
In every deft caress,
A concert seen through painter's eyes,
In mindful, soft finesse.

Symphony in oil unfolds,
In vibrant, fluid lines,
A concert that the heart beholds,
In swirls and elegant designs.

Mosaic of Emotions

Pieces of our heart and soul,
In fragments finely placed,
Every joy and every goal,
In patterns interlaced.

Shards of laughter, tears of night,
Come together, side by side,
Creating beauty in the light,
Where scattered dreams abide.

In sorrow's depth and bliss's height,
Our lives are gently spun,
Each emotion's colored light,
A spectrum soft as sun.

Moments sharp and moments soft,
In a mosaic spread so wide,
From the earth and from aloft,
Our feelings cannot hide.

A masterpiece of hope and fear,
In pieces small and vast,
This mosaic ever near,
A testament to all we've cast.

Silken Narratives

In threads of silk, tales unfold,
Ancient stories softly told,
Weave and warp in gentle dance,
Whispers of a lost romance.

Fibers blend in twilight hues,
Midnight whispers, morning dews,
Patterns weave through time and space,
Echoes of a silken grace.

Delicate and finely spun,
Shadows of the setting sun,
Every strand a tale complete,
Joined together, fond and sweet.

Artistry in fingers' touch,
Skillful move that says so much,
In the fabric, life is shown,
Silent tales forever sown.

Crafted wisdom in each thread,
Where the heart and soul have bled,
Silken narratives enfold,
Stories timeless to behold.

Stitches of Creativity

Needle dances through the night,
Crafting dreams in fabric's light,
Stitches form in rhythmic flow,
Creative sparks begin to glow.

Thread by thread, a masterpiece,
Ends and edges never cease,
Colors blend in perfect hue,
Visions old and visions new.

Textures speak in silent tones,
Creating worlds in unknown zones,
Patterns tell of inner sight,
Crafting day and endless night.

Every stitch a whispered vow,
Built with love, here and now,
Creative tides ever rise,
Seeing through the artist's eyes.

In the blend of thread and cloth,
Lies the spirit never lost,
Stitches of creativity,
Shape the world, set it free.

Ebb and Flow of Paint

Brush in hand, a stroke anew,
Canvas greets each vibrant hue,
Colors merge like rivers run,
Beneath the glowing, setting sun.

Ebb and flow in liquid grace,
Splashes find a tender place,
Vivid forms take gentle shape,
Dreams and memories escape.

Palette whispers secret shades,
Every layer softly fades,
In the strokes, emotions pour,
Onto parchment, evermore.

Fluid movement, art's embrace,
Time stands still in painted space,
Till the final touch is done,
Silent songs of color spun.

On the canvas, life does bloom,
Captured moments in the room,
Ebb and flow, the painter's plight,
Crafting daylight, birthing night.

Textured Whispers

Softly weave the twilight threads,
Whispers from the twilight beds,
Textures sing in muted tones,
Holding secrets, ancient stones.

Fingers trace the gentle lines,
Woven tales of silent signs,
In the touch, a story grows,
Quiet as the river flows.

Patterns speak in hushed delight,
Crafting dreams in shadowed night,
Every fiber tells a tale,
Whispers echo, never pale.

Textures weave the heart's desires,
In the loom of hidden fires,
Silent songs of time and place,
Woven with a tender grace.

In the dance of thread and string,
Lie the whispers stories bring,
Textured whispers, softly spun,
Till the final weave is done.

Embroidery of Dreams

In a realm where whispers weave,
Tales of fabric softly cleave,
Patterns birthed from silent seams,
Embroidery of our dreams.

Needles dance through twilight haze,
Crafting stars in silver maze,
Threads of fate in colors span,
Stitched by gentle, unseen hands.

Night's embrace with tender care,
Binds our hopes in moonlit air,
Each thread pulses, life imbues,
In this dream our spirits fuse.

Hues of dawn bleed into sky,
On this canvas dreams will fly,
With each patterned sigh and beam,
We live through embroidery of dreams.

Chisels and Threads

In the hands of those who mold,
Shape and form their stories told,
Chisels kiss the marble cold,
Whispers from the art unfold.

Threads of gold and silver bright,
Weave their tales in softest light,
Crafted by a skillful spin,
Merging where our souls begin.

Chiseled stone and woven cloth,
Speak of beauty, hearts enthralled,
Each with texture, depth, and grace,
Echoes of a dream's embrace.

In this art, our worlds unite,
Chisels, threads, a shared delight,
Patterns, forms in hues conveyed,
Craft our spirits, unafraid.

Textures of Creation

From the heart, a spark ignites,
Craftsmen weave both days and nights,
Textures of the world we see,
Patterns wild and colors free.

Hands that carve and hands that sew,
Bring to life what visions show,
Every stroke and every weave,
Part of stories we believe.

Sculpted lines and layers spun,
Underneath the rising sun,
Leaves a mark, a lasting trace,
Textures that our worlds embrace.

Each creation shares a voice,
In its form, the heart's rejoice,
Crafted with both love and fire,
Textures of our soul's desire.

Brushstrokes and Fibers

With each brushstroke, worlds appear,
Tales conveyed both bold and clear,
Colors blend in fluid streams,
Crafting visions, threading dreams.

Fibers spun from nature's loom,
In the artist's studio bloom,
Textures meet with painted flair,
Whispers of creation's care.

Brush and thread in harmony,
Join to form this tapestry,
Where designs in layers lie,
Stories woven through the eye.

Artists with both thread and paint,
Crafts their worlds, without constraint,
In each stroke and fiber's song,
Echoes of our spirits long.

Heritage in Stitches

Threads of yesterday, woven tight,
In patterns old, yet pure delight.
From hands long gone, they whisper still,
Soft echoes from the artist's will.

Colors blend in storied hues,
Each stitch a tale our hearts imbue.
Vintage hands worked dawn to night,
Creating heirlooms of pure might.

A legacy of fabric spun,
In every seam, traditions run.
Passed through ages, needle's song,
Crafts a history, proud and strong.

In quilts and garments, love is sewn,
With every piece, our past is known.
Heritage in thread and lace,
Time's embrace in every space.

These relics rest in sacred place,
Stitches holding love's embrace.
A tapestry of lives before,
Woven tight forevermore.

Portraits in Fiber

Within the weave, a face appears,
In strands of wool, erased the years.
An artist's touch on linen ground,
Silent stories, love unbound.

Each fiber spun with tender care,
Portraits vivid, stories rare.
Threads of memory, woven threads,
Bridging time with needleheads.

Eyes that gaze with timeless grace,
Captured in a woven face.
Textile dreams in colors vast,
Images of a bygone past.

Hands that brushed with cloth refined,
Crafting echoes, hearts entwined.
In fibers, human essence gleams,
Preserving moments, weaving dreams.

Portraits wrought by skilled design,
Lives immortal in each line.
In every thread, a story rests,
Portraits in fiber, love's behest.

Artful Looms

Upon the loom, the yarn takes flight,
Colors dance in pure delight.
Patterns form in graceful ease,
Crafted by the weaver's tease.

Threads entwine in grand array,
Daylight blends to twilight's gray.
Every shuttle's rhythmic call,
Weaves a tale which time enthralls.

Hands so skilled, they guide the flow,
In vibrant hues, the stories grow.
Artful looms, they sing with soul,
Creating tapestries whole.

With each pass, a story's spun,
In daylight's spark or morning's sun.
Threads of life and strands of dreams,
Woven through the warp and beams.

Heritage in threads refined,
Artful looms of every kind.
Past and future, mingled tight,
In woven art, our hearts take flight.

Sewn Legacies

Across the quilt, the patches fall,
In every stitch, a whispered call.
Hands that labored, hearts that cared,
In fabric's fold, love is shared.

Generations pass the needle,
Binding dreams both slight and feeble.
In seams so strong, the tales are told,
Sewn legacies from days of old.

Patterns deft from mind to cloth,
Memories interwoven, soft.
Family trees in stitches climb,
In woven knots, we trace the time.

With each seam, a tale unfolds,
Bound by threads in gentle molds.
Textile tales with love's embrace,
In every fabric, time and place.

From quilt to garment, bonds are made,
In every thread, dreams cascade.
Sewn legacies of hearts combined,
In fabric's stretch, our roots defined.

Dyed Dimensions

In hues of dreams, the fabric spins,
Weaving through the dark and light.
Secrets whisper from within,
Threads that dance in endless night.

Colors twist in boundless arcs,
Painted skies of fleeting time.
Dimensional and laced with sparks,
Rhythms in a silent chime.

Mystic shades in vibrant breaths,
Spectrum's pulse on vivid tide.
Patterns brushed by ancient depths,
Truths in woven myths reside.

Cerulean waves kiss the dawn,
Amber glows in twilight's gleam.
Infinite and gently drawn,
Worlds created in a dream.

Textured skies, the cosmos bends,
Ethereal realms, a mystic quest.
In dimensions, will it end?
Or in the weave, shall we rest?

Tangling Talents

Sylvan notes on breezes drift,
Cultivated arts entwine.
Talents weaving through the rift,
Threads of human hearts combine.

Poetry in every stroke,
Canvas breaths in vivid hues.
Tacit gifts stirred and awoke,
Crafted hands shape diverse views.

Symphonies in fingers stream,
Melodies in movements twist.
Every granting life a theme,
In the grace of artists kissed.

Angular in sculptor's dream,
Forms emerge in hewn embrace.
Mysteries of crafted seam,
Mirrored light on nature's face.

In such tangles, talents thrive,
Crafting beauty, pure and grand.
Through these ties, our spirits rive,
Wonders woven by our hand.

Patterns of Perception

Reality's prism bends the light,
Mirrors of our minds' creation.
Shapes and forms in shadows' flight,
Patterns of our contemplation.

Riddles cast in moon's embrace,
Silent tales of ages past.
Shifting truths in hidden place,
Mystic scripts in shadows cast.

Contours meld in twilight's sway,
Dreams and whispers intertwine.
Chasing echoes of the day,
Sight evolves where thoughts align.

Woven threads in mental streams,
Cognitive, the paths we trace.
In the labyrinth of dreams,
Patterns shift, yet still embrace.

In perception's vast expanse,
Every view a mirrored gleam.
Patterns change in cosmic dance,
Truth awakes in twilight's beam.

Imaginary Fabric

Dreams are stitched in fantasy,
Ephemeral threads that bind.
Fabrics born of endless sea,
    Tapestries of the mind.

Whispers trace the woven nooks,
    Fantasy's eternal loom.
Tales entwine in hidden books,
Realms of whispering bloom.

Patchwork skies where stars align,
Silent whispers weave the night.
Moonlit threads in lines entwine,
Mystic realms of endless light.

Minds enrapt in ancient lore,
Every stitch a world unfolds.
Fiction's fabric to explore,
    History in threads retold.

Imaginary warp and weft,
    Infinite in varied hue.
Magic in each corner left,
Waiting for the heart that flew.

Layered Impressions

Upon the canvas of the mind,
Dreams and shadows intertwine,
Layers of thoughts, so refined,
Crafting tales that time may find.

In whispers of the evening breeze,
Stories form in subtle lines,
Like footsteps in the autumn leaves,
Echoes weave through ancient pines.

Beneath the stars, silent and bright,
Illusions dance, worlds unfurl,
Soft brushstrokes in the moonlit night,
Layered impressions gently swirl.

Through memories, both old and new,
Emotions paint a vivid scene,
Each feeling, like the morning dew,
A moment captured, pure, serene.

In these depths, where senses play,
Truths and fancies blend and curl,
In the realm of dusk and day,
Layered dreams forever twirl.

Tactile Fantasies

Fingers trace the silken thread,
Through realms of touch and tender dreams,
Textures of a world widespread,
Stirred by more than what it seems.

In the softness of a whispered touch,
Cloth and skin in tender weave,
Sense awakens, feeling much,
Every fiber, thoughts conceive.

Velvet, satin, rough and smooth,
Tangible tales beneath the hand,
In every grain, emotions soothe,
Textures speak where words may stand.

Through the fabrics of our days,
Patterns of our stories spin,
Feeling shapes the nuanced ways,
Of the world we hold within.

In this tactile reverie,
Dreams are felt, not merely seen,
Through each touch, a fantasy,
Woven in a timeless sheen.

Translucent Weaves

Through gossamer, sunlight spills,
Threads of gold in gentle flow,
Forms emerge from misty thrills,
In translucent weaves, they grow.

Whispered secrets glide and blend,
Curtains of a dawn anew,
In the morning light, they send,
Echoes of a world in view.

Through veils thin, yet deeply felt,
Wonders of the heart exposed,
Hidden realms where shadows dwelt,
In their grace, a dream is posed.

Pale glimmers through the twilight reign,
Soft encounters, ghostly bright,
In their dance, an ancient strain,
Guides us through the silent night.

In these fragile, silken threads,
Life and dreams together weave,
Translucent paths where hope treads,
Mirrored whispers, we believe.

Embroidery of Dreams

Stitch by stitch, a story told,
Colors bright and threads entwine,
Dreams in patterns, bold and gold,
On life's fabric, finely line.

Each needle's touch, a vision spun,
In the night, dreams softly gleam,
Tapestries of what's begun,
In the realm of moonlit dreams.

Patterns weave through heart and soul,
Histories and futures blend,
In this art, we find our goal,
Moments pieced that never end.

Embroidery of sky and sea,
Starry nights and morning beams,
Every hue, a mystery,
In the threaded web, it seems.

In this dance of woven strands,
Life's great tale is deftly sewn,
With each stitch, our spirit stands,
In the dreams we've always known.

Interlaced Ideas

Threads of thought, so intricate and fine,
Weave a tapestry of elaborate design.
Concepts merge, knotting with ease,
Creating patterns that gently please.

Ideas twist like vines entwined,
Each one fresh, uniquely defined.
In the loom of a fertile mind,
Genius and madness are aligned.

Every thread a story told,
In colors bold or unbowed gold.
Interlaced in endless scheme,
A dream within a living dream.

Spindles spin and needles dance,
In a melancholic, rhythmic trance.
With every stitch, a bridge is spanned,
Forming worlds by steady hand.

In a cosmos of thought laid bare,
Interlaced ideas flare.
A radiant quilt of mental hue,
Woven with threads old and new.

Crafted by Hand

Each stroke of brush, a touch divine,
Shapes the world in hues benign.
Crafted by hand, with love and care,
Art born from fingers, light and fair.

Clay and stone, wood and sand,
Yield to artist's deft command.
From raw material, a vision springs,
Given life by tender things.

With fingers calloused, heart ablaze,
Creation sings in myriad ways.
Every piece a master's song,
A silent voice, though time prolongs.

In the labor, secrets lie,
In each crack and wrinkle plyed.
A testament to skill and strife,
Handcrafted for eternal life.

Man and material, bound by thread,
In works of wonder widely spread.
Born in sweat and often tears,
Crafted by hand to last through years.

Hued Stitches

Colors dance on fabric's plane,
In stitches hued, they bring terrain:
A meadow green, a sky so blue,
A sunset stitched in every hue.

Each thread a stroke in painter's hold,
Crafting tales in tints so bold.
Hued stitches speak without a sound,
Of beauty stitched on common ground.

From dyes extracted, hue by hue,
A world reborn in textures new.
Needles glide through woven dreams,
Creating visions, scarce it seems.

In every clothe a story spun,
Of battles lost and victories won.
With hued stitches deftly sewn,
The fabric breathes, the past is shown.

In the quiet of a needle's prance,
A dance of color, sweet romance.
Through patches mended, seams unfrayed,
Lives a legacy, brightly displayed.

Fiber Stories

Each strand bears tales from long ago,
Of distant lands and whispered woe.
Fiber stories interweave,
Of love and loss, of reprieve.

In ancient looms, the yarn is cast,
Spinning fables meant to last.
A legacy in twisted threads,
In fabric where the lore embeds.

With every wave of shuttle's flight,
Emerges dawn, dispels the night.
Fiber stories tell the past,
In colors bright and shadows vast.

With hands that deftly guide the loom,
Crafting tales in growing bloom.
In each knot a sentence lies,
A tale beneath the surface hides.

From sheep's coat to finished skein,
From grounded flax to silken gain.
Fiber stories, rich and grand,
Woven by a master's hand.

Entwined Inspirations

Beneath the morning's gentle sway,
Dreams awaken, come what may.
Threads of thought, in sunlight spun,
Weave ideas till the day is done.

Whispers soft on breezes glide,
Inspiration's voice, our faithful guide.
Paths untrodden, steps we tread,
Painted visions in the mind's spread.

Sun and shadow, hand in hand,
Designs of fate, so strong, so grand.
By hearts combined, tales unfold,
In silken words, their warmth to hold.

Mountains rise where valleys dream,
Rivers flow with hope's bright gleam.
Songs of time, through ages ring,
Entwined destinies, in chorus sing.

Moments fleeting, etched in space,
Lines and colors interlace.
Endless muse, our lives impress,
In inspirations, we find success.

Artful Knit

With needles swift, the yarn is cast,
Patterns form, from memories past.
Every stitch, a tale to tell,
From rise of dawn to twilight's bell.

Threads of life in colors bright,
Woven dreams through silent night.
Hands of time, in deft embrace,
Knit the world, a warm, tight space.

Tapestry in hues profound,
In each loop, a story's found.
Mystic symbols, crafted fine,
In woolen strands, the art entwine.

Seasons shift, yet steadfast still,
Craft of heart, the soul to fill.
Fabrics soft, with love and grace,
Each knitted piece, a warm embrace.

Eternal dance of needle, thread,
In every skein, a life is bred.
Artful knit, the gift of time,
In every row, a rhythmic rhyme.

Tangled Harmonies

Strings of life, so finely tuned,
Tunes of joy and sorrows crooned.
Entwined chords, in harmony,
Echoes ripple across the sea.

Melodies in twilight's grasp,
Notes in gentle whispers clasp.
Symphonies of hearts, they blend,
Tangled harmonies never end.

Fingers glide on ivories white,
Soul's expression, pure delight.
Harmony in every key,
In music, unbound spirits free.

Rhythms pulse beneath the stars,
Distant echoes of guitars.
Unified in song's embrace,
Harmony, a timeless space.

Silence too, a part does play,
In pauses, meanings find their way.
Tangled harmonies resound,
In quiet moments, truth is found.

Palettes of Passion

Brush of fire on canvas bare,
Colors dance with fervent flair.
Strokes of love, in vibrant shades,
Palettes of passion, sweet cascades.

Waves of crimson, waves of gold,
Emotions raw, in hues unfold.
Art's embrace in twilight's glow,
Through pigments pure, the feelings flow.

Mingling tones in soft caress,
Depths of heart in strokes confess.
Every line, a story's birth,
In painted whispers, art finds worth.

Textures rich in light and dark,
Flames of life ignite their spark.
Palettes blend in endless chase,
Eternal love on canvas trace.

Human form and nature's brawn,
In endless dance till night is dawn.
Palettes of passion, true and bright,
In every shade, love takes flight.

Crafted Echoes

In hands of skill, where magic flows,
Old tales revive, where history grows.
Each thread a story, each stitch a dream,
Crafted echoes in fabric's gleam.

Patterns emerge, like whispers past,
Timeless art, forever to last.
Silent songs in the weaver's hands,
Echoes of old, in modern lands.

Every motion, a legacy claimed,
Through humble work, artisans famed.
Threads entwined, in the loom's soft hum,
Silent echoes, where they come from.

Colors blend in vibrant dance,
In textile's weave, where dreams enhance.
Silent tales, through ages long,
Crafted echoes in fabric's song.

From loom and needle, to garment's form,
A world of history, rich and warm.
Echoes crafted, in every seam,
Whispers ancient, as silent dreams.

Threads of Imagination

In the mind's eye, with needles bright,
Threads of imagination take flight.
Colors dance, in patterns planned,
Stories woven by creative hand.

Ideas bloom in every thread,
A tapestry where dreams are spread.
From simple yarns, visions arise,
Crafted worlds before our eyes.

Each stitch a journey, each loop a tale,
Imagination in every detail.
Threads conjure, designs appear,
Crafted wonders, vivid and clear.

Patterns formed in thoughtful trance,
Imagination's bold expanse.
Through fabric's weave, new worlds unfold,
Stories waiting to be told.

In stitches fine, creation's thread,
Imagination duly fed.
Threads that bind both mind and art,
Woven dreams from the creative heart.

Handmade Tales

Needle and thread, a storyteller's tools,
Crafting tales beyond measured rules.
Fingers move with practiced grace,
Handmade tales, in fabric's embrace.

Each stitch a word, each seam a line,
In every thread, stories entwine.
Crafted tales of joy and strife,
Woven moments of life's own life.

Fabric whispers secrets kept,
In patterns where memories are swept.
Handmade tales of old and new,
Softly told, in colors true.

Building worlds in elegant skein,
Threads of gold, of joy and pain.
Handmade tales, both large and small,
In fabric form, they tell it all.

Crafted by heart, in every Fold,
Timeless tales, in stitches told.
Handmade art, so rich and hale,
In threads, the world's most cherished tale.

Textile Harmonies

In woven threads, a harmony pure,
Textile symphonies that allure.
Colors blend in perfect score,
Textile harmonies forever more.

Soft whispers in the fabric's song,
A melody, enduring, strong.
Each thread a note in gentle play,
Creating symphonies day by day.

Patterns flow with studied grace,
Textile tales in every place.
Harmony found in woven beams,
A silent choir of crafted dreams.

Every weave, a measured pace,
Textile harmonies find their space.
Tones of color, chords of thread,
A beautiful song, finely spread.

In the loom's embrace, a tune is born,
Textile harmonies, night and morn.
A fabric chorus, both loud and clear,
Singing to all who hold it dear.

Crafted Whimsy

In threads of laughter, dreams are spun,
Tangled tales have just begun.
With needles bright, daylight's theme,
Crafted whimsy, like a dream.

Fingers dance in patterns light,
Weave the magic of the night.
Softly whisper through the yarn,
Stories woven, never torn.

Each stitch binds, desires unfold,
Threads of silver, threads of gold.
From the spindle, webs take flight,
Chasing echoes in the light.

Framing fantasies in hue,
Crafted whimsy, ever new.
Every fabric tells a tale,
In this art, hearts will prevail.

As we knit our dreams in line,
Yarn and soul do intertwine.
In the loom, our hopes reside,
Crafted whimsy, side by side.

Artistic Entanglements

Colors blend in vibrant streams,
Collide in kaleidoscope dreams.
Canvas whispers secret ties,
Artistic eyes can't disguise.

Brushstrokes dance in swirling fates,
Whilst passion patiently waits.
Bound by cords of heart and mind,
Truth in tangles we shall find.

Poetry in every hue,
Artistic entanglements pursue.
Lines and shades in complex play,
Create the night, unveil the day.

In the chaos, lessons take,
Every knot a fervent sake.
Pictures forged in unity,
Rooted in complexity.

Uniqueness in each tangled thread,
By heartfelt visions gently led.
Artistic minds thus intertwined,
In creations we are defined.

Interwoven Colors

A spectrum born of woven light,
In tapestry, both day and night.
Interwoven colors speak,
In every hue, secrets peek.

Threads of crimson, threads of blue,
Bonding hearts in moments true.
Golden weaves of dreams unfold,
Interlacing tales untold.

Emerald greens of nature's pride,
Whispers of oceans deep and wide.
Within fibers, truths recall,
Interwoven by them all.

Patterns merge, and spirits blend,
In colors, letters do transcend.
Crafting life in vibrant streams,
Interwoven into dreams.

As life's tapestry takes form,
Moments soft and moments warm.
In this art, our souls find rest,
Interwoven, at our best.

Knots of Passion

In the shadows, dreams are caught,
Knots of passion, deeply sought.
Every loop and twist a spark,
In the heart, ignites a mark.

Fingers skilled in love's embrace,
Crafting whispers, silk and lace.
Binding threads that softly yearn,
Knots of passion gently burn.

Through the tangled strands we find,
Connections strong and intertwined.
Hearts entangled, minds entwined,
In each knot, our spirits bind.

Knots of passion, secrets told,
Stories bright, in strands of gold.
Weaving love in patterns fine,
Echoes last through webs of time.

With every twist, emotions flare,
In tender bindings, souls declare.
Knots of passion, bold yet sweet,
In each thread, our lives complete.

Artistry Interlaced

Threads of color, interwoven dreams,
Brushes whisper in silent streams,
Palette dances, hues collide,
Gift of vision, artist's pride.

Canvas breaths with every stroke,
Lines of beauty, tales invoke,
In the abstract, truth is traced,
Artistry in time embraced.

Mystic patterns, souls entwined,
Whispers sound within the mind,
Crafting realms with deft refrains,
Wrought in joy, born from pains.

Paint does speak, the heart's desire,
Fuel the passion, spark the fire,
Each creation, voice displayed,
Artistry, forever stayed.

Glimmered light and shadowed night,
Cradle dreams held soft and tight,
Art constructed, ever spaced,
Artistry, by time interlaced.

Canvas Crochet

Hands of yarn, deftly weave,
Patterns bloom, as hearts believe,
Fabric whispers, tales unfold,
Dreams of warmth, stories told.

Colors whisper, laced in thread,
Wishes caught in winding spread,
Knitting hearts with each connect,
Loving ties, souls reflect.

Patterns dance in crafted light,
Crochet dreams take tender flight,
Fingers craft with gentle care,
Love and patience, treasures rare.

Designs spun with thread so fine,
Weaving hopes in every line,
Canvas breathes, alive, complete,
Crochet dreams, ever sweet.

In the quiet, stitches flow,
Handmade worlds begin to grow,
Canvas sighs, the tales portray,
Crochet wonders, night and day.

Imagined Fabrics

Threads of thought, connection raw,
Imagined fabrics, minds do draw,
Tactile dreams in realms unknown,
Vision spun, creation sown.

Silken whispers, textured day,
Dreamscapes sewn, in deft display,
Patterns merging, dreams unite,
Fabric spun, the starry night.

Mental looms, ideas weave,
Magic spells, we both believe,
Tapestry, the soul's desire,
Crafted dreams, lifting higher.

Every thread, a thought's embrace,
Woven tight with utmost grace,
Embroidery of heart and mind,
Imagination, intertwined.

Fabrications, shared delight,
Warming souls in covers might,
Imagined worlds within our grasp,
Fabrics spun, in love holds fast.

Sculpted Textures

Stone and clay in master's hand,
Dreams take shape, by touch command,
Chisel whispers, marble sings,
Forms of life, creation brings.

Textures rise, await their birth,
Crafted from the earth's own worth,
Sculpted whispers, deep and true,
Emerging forms, they feel anew.

Contours grace the artist's sight,
Breathing forms from day to night,
Every carving, story frames,
Sculpted life, no art the same.

Hands of time in stone enshrined,
Crafting beauty, soul refined,
Textures speak where words would fail,
Silent tales, by hands unveiled.

Stone-heart whispers, clay's embrace,
Carved in time, with gentle grace,
Sculpted textures, life expressed,
Art of earth, forever blessed.

Threads of Expression

In the loom of twilight's gentle care,
Crafted stories weave the air.
Each fiber speaks in whispered strands,
Binding dreams with tender hands.

Colors merge in night's embrace,
Hidden secrets, threads retrace.
Silent looms, their tales unfurl,
Whispers from another world.

Threads of hope and threads of sorrow,
Intertwined in dawn's tomorrow.
Patterns shape the unseen layers,
Prayers stitched by unseen players.

Every loop a passage found,
In webs of fate, hope is bound.
Strings that bridge the silent lands,
Woven by unseen, patient hands.

In this fabric, lives entwine,
Delicate, divine design.
Marking time with each caress,
A tapestry of souls expressed.

Draped in Pigments

Canvas spreads in dawn's first light,
Brushes dance in skies of white.
Every stroke a voice unspoken,
Dreams in colors, gently woken.

Pallets sing in silent hues,
Whispers told in reds and blues.
Echoes trapped in vibrant scenes,
Lost in swirls of pastel dreams.

Oceans captured, forests stay,
In the strokes of every day.
Mountains rise where shadows fall,
Pigments tell the tale of all.

Azure skies and emerald seas,
Timeless tales on every breeze.
Crimson hearts and golden skins,
Painting life's unspoken whims.

Masterpieces born anew,
Worlds created from the blue.
Draped in pigments, souls entwine,
Art, the language so divine.

Artisan's Blessing

With skilled hands and thoughtful gaze,
Crafting life in myriad ways.
From raw stone to polished gem,
Nature's artistry through them.

Every chisel, every tool,
Breathes a spark from start to rule.
Wood and metal, clay and stone,
Under touch, they find a home.

Whispers from the ancient earth,
Echoes of forgotten worth.
Each creation tells a tale,
Timeless in its bold detail.

Blessed by seasons, time confined,
In each work, a soul defined.
Craftsmen shape with tender hands,
Dreams that span through distant lands.

Artisan's gift, a silent song,
Heartfelt, pure, and ever strong.
From their craft, a world adorned,
Life's sweet melodies reborn.

Ink and Yarn

Inked pages whisper, looms reply,
Stories twine as moments fly.
Words and threads in tandem tell,
Life's rich tapestry, pure and well.

Quills and needles poised in grace,
Crafting tales in time and space.
Letters dance and patterns weave,
In their art, the hearts believe.

Papyrus and the silken thread,
Voices live where once were dead.
Colors melt in inked embrace,
Truth and dreams they interlace.

From the ink's darkened spill,
Through the yarn's sweetened thrill.
Woven tales in text and thread,
Where the mind and heart are fed.

In these strands of ink and yarn,
Life and art forever drawn.
Words and fiber, tale entwined,
In their weave, the soul aligned.

Tangled Expressions

In the labyrinth of thoughts we drift,
Silver sparks in night's dark gift.
Echoes of whispers, lost and found,
In memories' threads, tightly wound.

Words spill like stars across the sky,
Painting tales as moments fly.
Fractured verses, intricate and free,
We carve our truths in tangled spree.

Through the veils of fleeting time,
Silent echoes weave and rhyme.
Dreams emerge from shadowed haze,
In tangled dance, through life's maze.

Eyes meet in the woven street,
Silent stories, bittersweet.
Paths diverge, yet still they cling,
To threads of fate and what they bring.

Love ignites in the twisted night,
Guided by the moon's soft light.
Mysteries in every strand,
Tangled expressions, hand in hand.

Fabric of Whimsy

In fields where dreams and wishes play,
Threads of laughter, light and gay.
Colors blend in playful streams,
Woven tales and whispered gleams.

Soft whispers in the wind afloat,
Carried on whimsy's delicate boat.
Patterns shift in gentle breeze,
A dance of stars among the trees.

Moments caught in the silken weave,
Stories old, new ones conceive.
In this tapestry of chance,
We find our way, in whimsy's dance.

Light and shadow, hand in hand,
Trace the lines on this vast land.
In the fabric of the night,
Mysteries unfold in flight.

Hearts entwine where shadows meet,
In the whimsy, life's heartbeat.
Dreams we tether to the sky,
In fabric woven, we comply.

Chromatic Weaves

Colors blend in twilight's glow,
Whispered secrets they bestow.
Chromatic weaves of silent dreams,
Flowing down the moonlit streams.

Ruby reds and sapphire blues,
Nature's palette, endless hues.
Stories painted on the breeze,
In every leaf and rustling tree.

Golden sun and emerald field,
Mysteries their shades reveal.
Through the prism of the soul,
Chromatic weaves make us whole.

Stitch by stitch the colors frame,
Our common joys, our unvoiced pain.
In the tapestry of time,
Every shade, every rhyme.

From dawn's first light to dusk's embrace,
Chromatic weaves our footsteps trace.
In the heartbeat of the world,
A vivid tale, unfurled.

Colorful Narratives

In the hues of morning light,
Stories born from darkest night.
Brushstrokes vast across the skies,
Colorful narratives, where truth lies.

Amber tales in twilight's glow,
Echoes of a past we know.
In the canvas of our days,
Life's vivid dance in endless plays.

Vermilion whispered through the breeze,
Secrets shared among the trees.
In the colors, we confide,
Dreams and hopes, side by side.

Canvas broad, the world our stage,
Every hue on every page.
Hearts and hands together weave,
Magic in the stories we believe.

In the rainbow's tender arch,
Stories etched in every march.
Colorful narratives, bold and true,
In every shade, a me and you.

Woven Masterpieces

Threads of gold and silver bright,
Interlace both day and night,
Stories told through woven art,
Fabric scenes that touch the heart.

Crafted with a steady hand,
Patterns rise at each command,
Every thread a tale retold,
Creating beauty, bold and old.

Weavers work with careful eye,
Shapes emerge by and by,
Colors blend and textures mold,
Artistry, a sight to behold.

From the loom, a world is born,
Rays of dawn to lines of morn,
Fingers dance, the threads comply,
Masterpieces by and by.

In the weave, we see the past,
Legacies made to last,
Art immortal in the thread,
Dreams and visions finely spread.

Stitches in Time

Needles pierce the fabric tight,
Drawing patterns through the night,
Every stitch a moment caught,
In this quilt of dreams and thought.

Seams they bind our memories,
Fastened tight eternities,
Through the cloth, our lives are spun,
Stitches tell of battles won.

Patches form a tapestry,
Of our shared humanity,
Every thread a tale unfurls,
In the fabric of the world.

Hands that work with tender care,
Weave the stories that we share,
From the old to yet unknown,
In each stitch, a seed is sown.

Quilts of life and time define,
Moments captured, threads align,
Pieces fit with fragile grace,
In the fabric, find our place.

Creative Tapestries

Colors burst from spools of thread,
Crafting visions in the head,
Every strand with purpose flows,
In the woven tale it shows.

Patterns form in grand display,
Textures blend in bold array,
Tales of wonder, joy and strife,
Woven in the cloth of life.

Each design a world apart,
Masterpieces born of art,
From the loom, creations sing,
Tapestries of everything.

Fingers guided by the mind,
Crafting stories, hearts entwined,
Through the weave, a life unfurled,
In the cloth, a mirrored world.

Art and heart together blend,
In each thread, a message send,
Crafted with meticulous care,
Creative tapestries declare.

Brush and Needle

Brush and needle, side by side,
Crafting worlds both far and wide,
Colors bold and threads so fine,
Painting pictures, stitch and line.

Canvas waits as needle glides,
Patterns form as art abides,
Every stroke and stitch combined,
In this dance of art entwined.

Brush strokes blend with needle's thread,
Creating something from what's bred,
Art and craft in unity,
Weaving vibrant harmony.

Hands that hold both tools with grace,
Summon beauty to this place,
On the canvas, stories told,
Brush and needle, heart and soul.

Work of passion, love and skill,
Every piece a window still,
Through the paint and thread we find,
Brush and needle, intertwined.

Woven Realities

In threads of wonder, dreams collide,
Tangled mystic, worlds untied,
Colors merge, a dance profound,
Woven realms in silence found.

Through gossamer strands, we trace,
Universes, face to face,
Patterns burst in cosmic light,
Daydream paths in darkest night.

Skies of azure, seas entwine,
Prodigies in shadow sign,
Winding trails, the heart discovers,
Canvas wide, the soul uncovers.

Each thread whispers past unknown,
Timeless tales by twilight sewn,
Fabric of existence worn,
Woven now, and yet reborn.

Mystery in every stitch,
Boundless paths where spirits switch,
Illusions mingling, clear and true,
Woven realms of me and you.

Tints of Tapestry

In hues of gold and emerald sheen,
Life unfolds within the scene,
Rich and deep, the colors hold,
Stories in their shadows bold.

Crimson streaks where passions flare,
Subtle shades of grace and care,
Every tint, a chapter spun,
Eloquent, our souls become.

Azure whispers, silent night,
Celestial songs in pale light,
Weaving tales of dreams yet seen,
Threads of what we might have been.

Scarlet hearts and violet peace,
Layers deep that never cease,
Ephemeral, the stories lie,
Tints of life beneath the sky.

In each brush, a life reborn,
Mosaic mind, by day forlorn,
Tales within the color spread,
Tints of tapestry, deeply fed.

Spiraling Hues

Swirling shades in cosmic dance,
Sight transcends in vibrant trance,
Patterns shift in endless move,
Hues that spiral, hearts approve.

Dizzy echoes, colors fall,
Cascading thoughts, within us all,
Rainbows bound in ribbon flux,
Flowing freely, breaking locks.

Twilight's serenade in bloom,
Midnight's hues in silken loom,
Colors chant in spirals bold,
Mystic stories we behold.

Emeralds twine with ruby reds,
In our dreams and in our beds,
Eternity in circles finds,
Spiraling hues in endless minds.

Unravelling, yet intertwine,
Magic born in every line,
Chromatic whispers, wondrous play,
Spiraling hues, by night and day.

Fibers of Vision

In strands of light, the truth unveils,
Future winds and ancient tales,
Weaving threads of hope and fear,
Vision bound where dreams adhere.

Fibers thin yet strong as stone,
Each a story, each alone,
Interlaced in grand design,
Encoded thoughts in patterns fine.

With every thread, a vision stirs,
Whispers of what was and heres,
Realms unknown and pasts embraced,
Fibers spun in subtle haste.

Cloth of life, in vision wide,
Warp and woof where fates reside,
Tapestry, our sight does bind,
Threads of future, shadows behind.

In the weave, our lives are held,
Mysteries, in colors swelled,
Fibers of vision, clear and true,
In the loom, are born anew.

Patchwork of Thoughts

A mosaic of moments, stitched in dreams,
Quilts of whispers, embroidered seams.
Fragments of memories, woven tight,
In the fabric of day, emerges night.

Patches of joy, sorrow's hem,
We trace the patterns, again and again.
Each thought a color, each word a thread,
In the quilt of life, where all is said.

Threads of gold, they shimmer bright,
Tales of love, in the tranquil light.
Stitches of pain, they too remain,
In the sprawling expanse, joy and pain.

Borders of silence, framed with grace,
In the endless quilt, I find my place.
Every patch a story, every line a song,
In the patchwork of thoughts, I belong.

The Painter's Lament

A canvas blank, a world unknown,
Brushes poised, dreams overgrown.
Colors whisper secrets in the night,
In the painter's heart, shadows and light.

Strokes of passion, vivid and wild,
Hues of despair, somber and mild.
In every shade, a tale unfolds,
A world of emotions, yet to be told.

The palette speaks of joys and fears,
Of silent glories, and unseen tears.
Each line a journey, each curve a thought,
In the painter's lament, battles are fought.

The easel groans with unspoken words,
In hues of blue, and silent chords.
Every stroke a sigh, every shade a plea,
In the painter's lament, the soul set free.

Crafting Reality

In shadows and light, dreams take shape,
From whispers of dawn, we forever escape.
Crafting a realm, both near and far,
In the heart's deep recess, a guiding star.

Words like clay, molded with care,
Truths and fables, hang in the air.
Realms unseen, with hands we make,
Each thought a fortress, yet to break.

Threads of time, woven with skill,
Moments of quiet, winds too still.
Crafted dreams, reality we see,
A dance of what is, and what must be.

In silent whispers, worlds unwind,
Crafted with love, both tender and kind.
In the hands of creators, the magic unfurls,
Reality itself, a series of worlds.

Tangled Inspirations

In the web of musings, thoughts entwine,
A labyrinth of whispers, serpentine.
Every corner, a spark, every turn a glow,
In tangled inspirations, ideas grow.

Threads of wonder, bound and frayed,
In the loom of mind, the colors displayed.
Every knot a struggle, every weave a burst,
In the tangled web, dreams immersed.

Wanderer of thoughts, seeker of light,
In the maze of musings, day and night.
Tangled inspirations, a beacon bright,
Guiding hearts in the endless flight.

The tapestry of musings, rich and vast,
A chronicle of dreams, from present to past.
Bound by thoughts, we create and find,
In tangled inspirations, heart and mind.

Patterns of Inspiration

In threads of thought, we weave the day,
Evolving paths where colors play.
Through trials and dreams, our spirits find,
The patterns etched within our mind.

Soft whispers call from distant lands,
Guiding hearts with gentle hands.
With every stitch, a story blooms,
In embroidered suns and silver moons.

Inspiration like a river flows,
A steady path through highs and lows.
Wings of hope in every thread,
Into endless skies, we're gently led.

From shadows deep to radiant light,
In ever-changing hues so bright.
The fabric of our lives unfurled,
Inspiration's dance across the world.

With needle fine and colors bold,
A tapestry of souls, untold.
The patterns of our hearts unspoken,
In every thread, a door's been opened.

Vivid Yarn Stories

Tales are spun in quiet nights,
From simple strings to glorious heights.
Each word a stitch in fabric fine,
Creating tapestries divine.

Colors of a past long gone,
Interwoven, moving on.
From legends told in fireside glow,
To truths that only dreamers know.

Through hands of old, through hearts anew,
The stories whisper, winding through.
In every yarn, a life preserved,
In every stitch, a voice is heard.

Dreams entwine with threads of gold,
Histories in patterns bold.
The dance of tales, forever spun,
A woven web, by many, one.

In each creation, joy and tears,
In every stitch, the passing years.
Thus, we tell, with hands and heart,
The vivid yarns from life apart.

Cultural Weavings

From every corner of the earth,
A tapestry of human worth.
Cultures blend as threads entwine,
In patterns intricate, divine.

In dance and song, in cloth and clay,
Stories old and new convey.
Through generations' hands and eyes,
Heritage in fabric lies.

Colors speak of lands afar,
Patterns like a guiding star.
Through weavings rich, our hearts explore,
The lives of those who came before.

Seamless threads of history,
A mosaic of mystery.
In cultural designs we find,
A unity of humankind.

A weave of voices, bright and true,
In every thread, a world anew.
From ancient looms to modern seams,
Cultural weavings mend our dreams.

Interlaced Visions

Visions interlaced with light,
Like stars that guide us through the night.
Threads of hope and dreams unleashed,
Every pattern, soul's motif.

Contours drawn on silky thread,
By dreams the heart and mind have fed.
Patterns formed in tranquil spaces,
Visions interlace through phases.

Each stitch a frame of foresight clear,
Through darkest night and day so dear.
In interlaced visions to see,
The life that was, and yet will be.

Festooned with colors, bold and bright,
In every thread, the purest light.
Crafted dreams in fabric shown,
In every weave, a world is grown.

Within each interlaced refrain,
A promise lies through joy and pain.
Visions crafted, shared, and mended,
By threads of dreams, our tales extended.

Hues of Existence

A canvas spread in endless scope,
With brushes dipped in dreams so deep,
The colors blend to forge our hope,
In every shade, our secrets keep.

Amber skies at dawn's first light,
Reflect the promise of the day,
Each hue a testament to might,
In life's grand art, we twine and sway.

Azure waves in oceans vast,
Hold echoes of our past and fears,
Yet in their depths, the die is cast,
Of laughter, love, and silent cheers.

Verdant fields where life takes root,
Whisper tales of growth and change,
In every sprout, the unquestioned truth,
That we evolve, and yet remain.

In this chromatic maze we wade,
Through twilight's shade and noon's bright glow,
We paint our steps in calm or raid,
In hues of life, ourselves we show.

Interlaced Visions

Threads of silk in twilight weave,
Form patterns in the waking dream,
Where visions interlace, conceive,
A tapestry both dark and gleam.

In lucid dreams, we walk on air,
With toes that never touch the ground,
Each scene a world beyond compare,
Where silent whispers have a sound.

Connecting minds across the vast,
Unseen, yet felt with every pulse,
Through corridors of future's past,
We journey with an inner impulse.

Eyes closed, yet seeing more than real,
Our senses bridge the space unseen,
In there, the heart begins to heal,
Where all is veiled, yet all is keen.

Cloaked in mist, these visions bind,
The waking life and dream's soft grace,
In interlaced thoughts, we find,
A mirrored self in endless space.

Woven Illusions

Illusions spun in silver threads,
Between the night and breaking dawn,
They whisper in our sleepy heads,
Of places seen yet quickly gone.

Reality in shadows plays,
A fickle dance of light and dark,
In every twist, the thread obeys,
The loom of fate leaves not a mark.

Mirages formed in desert heat,
Invite the mind to wander free,
Yet in their grasp, the heart must beat,
A rhythm bound by what might be.

Gossamer dreams on breezes fly,
Through tangled thoughts, they find their way,
In woven mists, life's truths belie,
The lines of night and edge of day.

In this web, we're all entwined,
With hopes and fears both bright and veiled,
Where woven illusions leave behind,
A soul's own tale, however frail.

Ethereal Touch

In moonlit realms, where shadows play,
A touch that's felt but leaves no trace,
The spirits dance in soft relay,
Enshrouded in their mystic grace.

With every breath, a whisper trails,
Through the veils of night, so fine,
Ethereal touch in dream prevails,
With stories told in silent sign.

We float on airs of pure delight,
In worlds unseen but deeply known,
Each touch a spark in endless night,
Through unseen hands, our seeds are sown.

A gentle breeze, a ghostly kiss,
In fleeting moments, hearts align,
An ethereal touch in boundless bliss,
Where mortal bounds forever pine.

Beyond the flesh, this touch endures,
Connecting souls in timeless bind,
In the ethereal, pure and sure,
We touch the infinite, entwined.

Chromatic Tapestry

Threads of gold and crimson weave,
In the twilight's gentle sleeve.
Colors dance in evening's light,
Crafting patterns, pure delight.

Emerald tendrils twist and spin,
Binding tales that lie within.
Whispers of the past and dreams,
In this fabric, nothing seems.

Azure skies with silver stars,
Stretch the canvas, wide and far.
Every hue, a story told,
In the weave, the heart unfolds.

Mysteries wrapped in threads so fine,
Each one unique, a pure design.
Harmony in every thread,
In this tapestry, life is read.

Crimson dawn and violet dusk,
In colors, trust is held in trust.
Boundless beauty, endless spree,
In chromatic tapestry.

Weaving the Spectrum

Colors blend in twilight's shade,
In this dance, no hue will fade.
Rainbow threads in union strong,
Create a symphony of song.

Indigo and lavender light,
Merge together, pure and bright.
Emerald greens and scarlet reds,
Bound in tales that never end.

Golden strands like rays of sun,
In this weave, all threads are one.
Cerulean dreams in satin streams,
Painted in the weaver's schemes.

Melodies in pigments spun,
In the threads where dreams are hung.
Weaving stories, life and lore,
In each strand, a world explored.

Every thread an endless spree,
Crafting worlds that set us free.
In this grand, chromatic stream,
Weaving the spectrum, dream by dream.

Brush of Silence

In the quiet of the night,
Brush of silence takes its flight.
Whispers on an unseen breeze,
Painting tales with gentle ease.

Every stroke a silent song,
In this hush where dreams belong.
Shades of stillness, soft and true,
Crafting visions ever new.

Canvas of the moonlit skies,
Holds the weight of quiet sighs.
Brush of silence, tender, slow,
Paints the dreams we come to know.

In the silence, colors gleam,
Bringing life to every dream.
Each soft stroke a story spun,
In the quiet, all is one.

Brush of silence, whispers sweet,
In the night where hearts do meet.
Crafting beauty in the night,
With each stroke, a tale of light.

Luminescent Fabrics

Woven light in threads so bright,
Luminescent fabrics' flight.
Glimmers of a distant star,
Caught in strands that travel far.

Celestial weaves in silver light,
Crafting patterns in the night.
Nebulas in hues arrayed,
In this fabric, dreams are made.

Cosmic dye in twilight's loom,
Interweaving space and bloom.
Threads of starlight, soft and sheer,
Cast away each doubt and fear.

Glowing threads in silent sway,
Dance in night, then greet the day.
Luminescent, pure and true,
In every thread, a world anew.

Shimmering paths in twilight's quilt,
In each fiber, dreams are built.
Bound in light where spirits roam,
Luminescent fabrics' home.

Milton Keynes UK
Ingram Content Group UK Ltd.
UKHW022119220724
445848UK00012B/176